D1065061

Wedding Anniversaries
from paper to diamond

Wedding Anniversaries

from paper to diamond

RYLAND
PETERS
& SMALL
LONDON NEW YORK

Cookie Lee

For my husband, Andrew Richard

First published in the United States in 2001
by Ryland Peters & Small, Inc.,
519 Broadway, 5th Floor
New York, NY 10012
www.rylandpeters.com
10 9 8 7 6 5 4 3 2

Design and photographs,
© Ryland Peters & Small 2001.
Text © Catherine Lee, 2001. Extracts of poetry
and prose are credited on page 64.
Special Photography Dan Duchars
Styling for Special Photography Rose Hammick

Printed and bound in China.

Library of Congress Cataloging-in-Publication Data
Lee, Cookie.
   Wedding anniversaries : from paper to diamond /
Cookie Lee.
   p. cm.
ISBN 1-84172-206-5
1. Wedding anniversaries. I. Title.
GT2800. L44 2001
394.2--dc21   2001031887

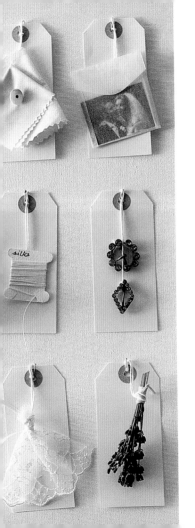

contents

Introduction

Marriage is a near universal experience. Most societies, cultures, and religions recognize it, and over many centuries, unique traditions, beliefs, and customs have grown up around marriage. Despite modern cynicism, changing social patterns, and the rejection of old-fashioned institutions, we are still choosing to "tie the knot" with our loved ones.

The tradition of marking the successful completion of a period of marriage with a special gift has survived largely through oral history. Each year, attention is paid to this old folklore custom, and relevant gifts are given to the couple. The anniversaries most generally observed and celebrated with presents and parties are the silver, ruby, golden, and diamond. Luckily, the tokens associated with the other anniversaries have charm without great cost and will inspire the perfect gift for those celebrating another year of marriage.

The meaning of the months of marriage

Married when the year is new

He'll be loving, kind and true

When February birds do mate

You wed nor dread your fate

If you wed when March winds blow

Joy and sorrow both you'll know

Marry in April when you can

Joy for maiden and the man

Marry in the month of May

And you'll surely rue the day

Marry when the June roses grow

Over land and sea you'll go

Those, who in July do wed

Must labour for their daily bread

Whoever wed in August be

Many a change is sure to see

Marry in September's shine

Your living will be rich and fine

If in October you do marry

Love will come, but riches tarry

If you wed in bleak November

Only joys will come, remember

When December's snows fall fast

Marry and true love will last.

Old English rhyme

first

May heaven grant you in all things your heart's desire—husband, house, and a happy peaceful home. For there is nothing better in this world than that a man and woman, sharing the same ideas, keep house together. It discomforts their enemies and makes the hearts of their friends glad—but they themselves know more about it than anyone.

Homer (8th century B.C.)

Love is, above all, the gift of oneself.

Jean Anouilh (1910–1987)

paper

second

Love one another, but make not a bond of love:

Let it rather be a moving sea between the shores of your souls.

Fill each other's cup but drink not from one cup.

Give one another of your bread but eat not from the same loaf.

Sing and dance together and be joyous, but let each

one of you be alone,

Even as the strings of a lute are alone though they quiver

with the same music.

Give your hearts, but not into each other's keeping.

For only the hand of Life can contain your hearts.

And stand together yet not too near together:

For the pillars of the temple stand apart,

And the oak tree and the cypress grow not in each other's shadow.

Kahlil Gibran (1883–1931)

cotton

third

To keep your marriage brimming,

With love in the loving cup,

Whenever you're wrong, admit it;

Whenever you're right, shut up.

Ogden Nash (1902–1971)

Who could relate, save those that wedded be,

The joy, the ease, and the prosperity

That are between a husband and a wife?

Geoffrey Chaucer (c1340–1400)

leather

fourth

Love is a fanclub with only two fans.

Adrian Henri (1932–2000)

Like fingerprints, all marriages are different.

George Bernard Shaw (1856–1950)

linen

traditional alternatives: fruit or flowers

fifth

Let me not to the marriage of true minds

Admit impediments. Love is not love

Which alters when it alteration finds,

Or bends with the remover to remove:

O, no! it is an ever-fixed mark,

That looks on tempests and is never shaken;

It is the star to every wandering bark,

Whose worth's unknown, although his height be taken.

Love's not Time's fool, though rosy lips and cheeks

Within his bending sickle's compass come;

Love alters not with his brief hours and weeks,

But bears it out even to the edge of doom.

If this be error and upon me proved,

I never writ, nor no man ever loved.

William Shakespeare (1564–1616)

wood

sixth

The supreme happiness in life is the conviction that we are loved.

Victor Hugo (1802–1885)

A married couple are well suited when both partners usually

feel the need for a quarrel at the same time.

Jean Rostand (1894–1977)

iron

seventh

7

Man is lyrical, woman epic, marriage dramatic.

Novalis (1772–1801)

It is not a lack of love, but a lack of friendship that makes unhappy marriages.

Friedrich Nietzche (1844–1900)

wool

eighth

I celebrate myself, and sing myself,

And what I assume you shall assume,

For every atom belonging to me as good belongs to you.

Walt Whitman (1819–1892)

All love that has not friendship for its base,

Is like a mansion built upon the sand.

Ella Wheeler Wilcox (1850–1919)

bronze

ninth

9

There is no happy life

But in a wife;

The comforts are so sweet

When they do meet.

Two figures but one coin;

So they do join,

Only they not embrace,

We face to face.

William Cavendish, Duke of Newcastle (17th century)

traditional alternative: copper

pottery

tenth

Marriage is popular because it combines the maximum

of temptation with the maximum of opportunity.

George Bernard Shaw (1856–1950)

That is why marriage is so much more interesting than divorce,

Because it's the only known example of the happy meeting of the

immovable object and the irresistible force.

So I hope husbands and wives will continue to debate and combat

over everything debatable and combatable,

Because I believe a little incompatibility is the spice of life.

Ogden Nash (1902–1971)

tin

eleventh

Chains do not hold a marriage together. It is threads, hundreds of tiny threads which sew people together through the years. That is what makes a marriage last—more than passion or even sex!

Simone Signoret (1921–1985)

What is a kiss? Why this, as some approve:
The sure, sweet cement, glue and lime of love.

Robert Herrick (1591–1674)

steel

twelfth

12

I ... chose my wife, as she did her wedding gown, not for a fine

glossy surface, but such qualities as would wear well.

Oliver Goldsmith (1728–1774)

A cigarette that bears a lipstick's traces,

An airline ticket to romantic places;

And still my heart has wings

Those foolish things

Remind me of you.

Holt Marvell (1901–1969)

silk

traditional alternative: linen

thirteenth

The great secret of a successful marriage is to treat all disasters

as incidents and none of the incidents as disasters.

Harold Nicolson (1886–1968)

At the touch of love, everyone becomes a poet.

Plato (c428–347)

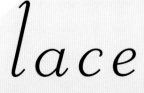

lace

fourteenth

"Thee, Mary, with this ring I wed,"

So, fourteen years ago, I said.

With that first ring I married youth,

Grace, beauty, innocence, and truth;

Here then, to-day—with faith as sure,

With ardour as intense and pure,

As when amidst the rites divine

I took thy troth, and plighted mine.

Those virtues which, before untried,

The wife has added to the bride.

Samuel Bishop (1731–1795)

ivory

fifteenth

Those who have never known the deep intimacy and the intense companionship of happy mutual love have missed the best thing that life has to give.

Bertrand Russell (1872–1970)

Let him kiss me with the kisses of his mouth: for thy love is better than wine.

Song of Solomon

crystal

twentieth

The ideal story is that of two people who go into love step for step, with a fluttered consciousness, like a pair of children venturing together into a dark room.

Robert Louis Stevenson (1850–1894)

Her gesture, motion and her smiles,

Her wit, her voice my heart beguiles,

Beguiles my heart, I know not why,

And yet I love her till I die.

Anon (17th century)

china

twenty-fifth

Life has taught us that love does not consist in gazing at each other, but in looking together in the same direction.

Antoine de Saint-Exupéry (1900–1944)

Had I as many hearts as hairs,

As many lives as lovers' fears,

As many lives as years have hours,

They all and only should be yours!

Anon (17th century)

silver

thirtieth

But now when autumn yellows all the leaves

And thirty seasons mellow our long love,

How rooted, how secure, how strong, how rich,

How full the barn that holds our garnered sheaves!

Vita Sackville-West (1892–1962)

There is no greater risk, perhaps, than matrimony, but

there is nothing happier than a happy marriage.

Benjamin Disraeli (1804–1881)

pearl

thirty-fifth

A belt of straw and ivy buds,

With coral clasps and amber studs,

And if these pleasures may thee move,

Come live with me, and be my love.

Christopher Marlowe (1543–1607)

Many waters cannot quench love, neither can the floods drown it.

Song of Solomon

coral

fortieth

It's many years since fust we met,

'Er 'air was then as black as jet,

It's whiter now, but she don't fret,

Not my old gal...

We've been together for forty years,

An' it don't seem a day too much,

There ain't a lady livin' in the land,

As I'd swap for my dear old Dutch.

Albert Chevalier (1861–1923)

ruby

forty-fifth

Love is patient and kind; love is not jealous or boastful;

it is not arrogant or rude.

Love does not insist on its own way; it is not irritable or resentful;

It does not rejoice at wrong, but rejoices in the right.

Love bears all things, believes all things, hopes all things, endures all things.

I Corinthians

sapphire

fiftieth

If ever two were one, then surely we.

If ever man were lov'd by wife, then thee;

If ever wife was happy in a man,

Compare with me ye women if you can.

I prize thy love more than whole Mines of gold,

Or all the riches that the East doth hold.

My love is such that Rivers cannot quench,

Nor ought but love from thee, give recompence.

Thy love is such I can no way repay,

The heavens reward thee manifold I pray.

Anne Bradstreet (c1612–1672)

gold

fifty-fifth

He's more myself than I am. Whatever our souls are made

of, his and mine are the same.

Emily Brontë (1818–1848)

The memories of long love gather like drifting snow, poignant as

the mandarin ducks who float side by side in sleep.

Murasaki Shikibu (c978–1031)

emerald

sixtieth

Only our love hath no decay;

This, no tomorrow hath, nor yesterday,

Running it never runs from us away,

But truly keeps his first, last, everlasting day.

John Donne (1572–1631)

traditional alternative:
platinum

diamond

Modern wedding anniversary symbols

For an alternative token of love, the following ideas incorporate the traditional and the contemporary...

1st	Clocks		14th	Gold jewelry
2nd	China		15th	Watches
3rd	Crystal, Glass		16th	Silver hollowware
4th	Appliances		17th	Furniture
5th	Silverware		18th	Porcelain
6th	Wood objects		19th	Bronze
7th	Desk sets		20th	Platinum
8th	Linens/Lace		21st	Brass/Nickel
9th	Leather goods		22nd	Copper
10th	Diamond		23rd	Silver plate
11th	Fashion jewelry		24th	Musical instruments
12th	Pearls/Colored gems		25th	Sterling silver
13th	Textiles/Furs		26th	Original pictures

27th	Sculpture	42nd	Improved real estate
28th	Orchids	43rd	Travel
29th	New furniture	44th	Groceries
30th	Diamond	45th	Sapphire
31st	Timepieces	46th	Original poetry tribute
32nd	Conveyances	47th	Books
33rd	Amethyst	48th	Optical goods
34th	Opal	49th	Luxuries of any kind
35th	Jade	50th	Gold
36th	Bone china	55th	Emerald
37th	Alabaster	60th	Diamond
38th	Beryl/Tourmaline	80th	Diamond/Pearl
39th	Lace	85th	Diamond/Sapphire
40th	Ruby		
41st	Land		

Some history . . .

The giving of gifts has long been associated with weddings and marriage. The word wedlock comes from the Anglo-Saxon word *wedlac*, "wed" (from the Old English *wedden*, related to the Greek *wetten*, to bet) meaning pledge and "lac," a gift. Both of these are believed to come from the Old Norse, *vethja*, also meaning to pledge. In other words, the gift given to cement an engagement.

Prior to 1937, only the 1st, 5th, 10th, 15th, 20th, 25th, 50th, and 75th anniversary had a material associated with it. In 1937, the American National Retail Jeweler Association issued a more comprehensive list, which associated a material for each anniversary year up to the 20th and then each fifth year after that up to the 75th, with the exception of the 65th.

Credits

Solange Azagury-Partridge
171 Westbourne Grove
London W11 2RS, England
t.+44 (0)20 7792 0198
Page: 50
Haute couture jewelry.

Gregory Bottley and Lloyd
13 Seagrove Road
London SW6 1RP, England
t.+44 (0)20 7381 5522
Page 54
Rock, mineral, and fossil
dealers.

Guinevere
574 King's Road
London SW6 2DY, England
t.+44 (0)20 7736 2917
Pages: 37 and 42
Exquisite antiques.

Dinny Hall
200 Westbourne Grove
London W11 2RH, England
t.+44 (0)20 7792 3913
www.dinnyhall.com
Page 57 and front jacket
Silver, gold and semi-
precious jewelry.

Mufti
789 Fulham Road
London SW6 5HD, England
t.+44 (0)20 7610 9123
Page: 15
Elegant range of home
furnishings.

Ann Shore
Designer & Stylist, England
By appointment only.
t./f.+44 (0)20 7377 6377
Page: 18
Eclectic mix of old and
new objects for sale.

Wright & Teague
1A Grafton Street
London W1S 4EB
t.+44 (0)20 7629 2777
www.wrightandteague.com
Page 53
Contemporary jewelry.

Virginia
98 Portland Road
London W11 4LQ, England
t.+44 (0)20 7727 9908
Page: 35
Vintage clothing.

Useful addresses

Anthropologie
375 West Broadway
New York NY 10012
t. 212 343 7070
www.anthropologie.com
Accessories, furniture, and
home decor inspired by
cultures around the world.

eluxury.com
www.eluxury.com
Luxurious gift ideas.

RedEnvelope Gifts Online
www.RedEnvelope.com
t. 877 733 3683
Ideal gifts online.

Takashimaya
693 Fifth Avenue
New York NY 10022
t. 212 350 0100
Global department store.

Tiffany & Co.
Fifth Avenue at 57th Street
New York NY 10022
t. 212 755 8000
www.tiffany.com
Jewelry and gifts.

Acknowledgments

First Homer, *The Odyssey, Book IV*. Jean Anouilh, *Ardèle* (Methuen Publishing Limited.)

Second Kahlil Gibran, *The Prophet*, Wordsworth Classics *of World Literature* (Wordsworth Editions Limited 1996.) Reprinted by permission of Wordsworth Editions Limited.

Third Ogden Nash, 'A Word to Husbands,' *Candy is Dandy*; (André Deutsch Limited 1994). Geoffrey Chaucer, 'The Franklin's Tale,' *The Canterbury Tales*.

Fourth Adrian Henri, *Love is ...* (Bloodaxe 1994.) George Bernard Shaw. Reprinted by permission of The Society of Authors on behalf of the Bernard Shaw estate.

Fifth William Shakespeare, Sonnet 116, 'Let me not to the marriage of true minds.'

Sixth Victor Hugo. Jean Rostand, *Le Marriage* (Hachette 1927.)

Seventh Novalis. Friedrich Nietzche.

Eighth Walt Whitman, 'Song of Myself.' Ella Wheeler Wilcox, 'Upon the Sand.'

Ninth William Cavendish, Duke of Newcastle.

Tenth George Bernard Shaw, *Man and Superman* (University Press 1903.) Reprinted by permission of The Society of Authors on behalf of the Bernard Shaw estate. Ogden Nash, 'I do, I will, I have,' *Candy is Dandy*, (André Deutsch Limited 1994.)

Eleventh Simone Signoret, in *Daily Mail* 4 July 1978. Robert Herrick, 'Kiss.'

Twelfth Oliver Goldsmith, *The Vicar of Wakefield*. Holt Marvell, 'These Foolish Things Remind Me of You,' (1935.)

Thirteenth Harold Nicolson. Reprinted by permission of Nigel Nicolson. Plato, *Symposium*.

Fourteenth Samuel Bishop, 'To his Wife on the Fourteenth Anniversary of her Wedding Day, with a Ring.'

Fifteenth Bertrand Russell, *Marriage and Morals*, (Routledge 1985.) Reprinted by permission of Routledge. 'Song of Solomon,' *The Bible*.

Twentieth Robert Louis Stevenson, 'El Dorado,' *Virginibus Puerisque*.

Twenty-fifth Antoine de Saint-Exupéry, *Wind, Sand and Stars* (1939.)

Thirtieth Vita Sackville-West, in Nigel Nicolson, *Portrait of a Marriage* (Weidenfeld & Nicolson 1973.) Reprinted by permission of Nigel Nicolson. Benjamin Disraeli, writing to Princess Louise on her engagement to the Marquess of Lorne.

Thirty-fifth Christopher Marlowe, 'The Passionate Shepherd to His Love.' 'Song of Solomon,' *The Bible*.

Fortieth Albert Chevalier.

Forty-fifth 'I Corinthians,' *The Bible*.

Fiftieth Anne Bradstreet, 'To My Dear and Loving Husband.'

Fifty-fifth Emily Brontë, *Wuthering Heights*. Murasaki Shikibu, *The Tale of Genju*.

Sixtieth John Donne, 'The Anniversary.'

Modern wedding anniversary symbols

Anderson, Charles, 'The Exchange,' RQ 25 (1985): 175. *The World Almanac and Books of Facts*, (World Almanac Books 1997). *World Book Encyclopedia*, (1997 ed.), s.v. "wedding anniversary." Source: Chicago Public Library Website.

The Author has made every effort to secure permission for works in copyright. The Publisher will be happy to amend any errors or omissions in future editions of the book.